The Anthony Zigler Guide to Time Travellers

(in handy alphabetical order)

by Anthony J Zigler (with a little help from Wendy Body)

illustrated by David Lock

I hope you have been able to put your machine together by now. I know it's not easy and I admit there have been problems in putting some of the bits together.

Well it went there yesterday, I know it did!

Planets you know about can be boring, so this guide won't tell you anything about them. (Hard luck if you want to know anything about the moon – you'll have to find another book.)

B is for Baby

Going back to visit yourself at the age of one can be interesting.

C is for Camera

Don't take a camera with you –
you can't take photos of the past or the future.

D is for Dinosaurs

Most of them were a lot bigger than you are, so it's best to keep your distance.

E is for Exit

Make a quick exit if you meet Tyrannosaurus Rex! Its teeth could give you a nasty nip!

F is for Favourite food

Mine happens to be jelly sandwiches
so I always take some with me.
Time travelling can be hungry work.

Ziggy? Oh he's making himself a little snack right now ...

G is for Greeks

The Ancient Greeks invented the Olympics so I always go to keep fit classes before travelling back to their time ...
not that it helps much.

H is for Help!

This is what you should shout if you are chased by a hairy mammoth. It won't do any good but you might feel better.
(On second thoughts, perhaps you should save your breath for running.)

I is for ILL!

This is what happens if you travel too fast – especially backwards.

K is for Key

The starter key for your time machine is very important. Do not lose it.

L is for Lunar Landing

Go back to 1969 and you can watch Neil Armstrong step onto the moon. Go forward to 2089 and you can step onto it yourself.

M is for Maintenance

This is very important if your time machine is to stay in good working order. That way you won't visit 1066 when you wanted to go to 9901.

N is for Never

NEVER forget where you parked your time machine. You may need to get to it in a hurry.

O is for Overcoat

You will need one if you go back to the Ice Age. (A hot water bottle would be handy, too.)

P is for Pyramids

You can visit the pyramids in the present or go back to Ancient Egypt and have all the fun of helping to build them.

Q is for Quiet rest

You'll need it if you've been helping to build the pyramids.

R is for Romans

The Romans went in for a lot of baths.
Take your swimsuit if you visit their time.

S is for the Stone Age

Chipping flints is rather boring,
but cave painting can be fun.

T is for Toothbrush and Toothpaste

YOU need these – but don't try using them on a sabre-toothed tiger!

Hold still, I'm only trying to clean your teeth!

U is for Umbrella

Past, present or future, you can bet it will rain! Umbrellas are also useful for other things ...

SIT!

V is for Vikings

They were a fierce lot who sailed the seas and loved a good fight. Do not try to hitch a ride on a longship.

X is for X-ray

Your Mark 5 Time Machine has an x-ray eye.
You will find this can be quite useful.

Y is for Yeti

These large shy creatures live in the Himalayas. They were not found until 2062 so it's no use visiting them before this date.

Z is for Zeglosaurus Futurus

Never met one? Well, you might if you travel forward to 3473!